FINANCIAL FREEDOM

Debt Management Plan

"It takes courage to grow up and become who you really are."
— E.E. Cummings

Wellness
Balance
Calmness
Mindset

"Your self-worth is determined by you. You don't have to depend on someone telling you who you are."
— Beyoncé

Be BRAVE

MAKE TODAY GREAT

I CAN DO IT

STAY INSPIRED

YES YOU CAN

KEEP IT SIMPLE

DO MORE OF WHAT MAKES YOU HAPPY.

PEACE

"Nothing is impossible. The word itself says 'I'm possible!'"
Audrey Hepburn

BE AUTHENTIC

JUST BE YOU

CELEBRATE

"Keep your face always toward the sunshine, and shadows will fall behind you."
— Walt Whitman

LOVE

"Attitude is a little thing that makes a big difference."
— <u>Winston Churchill</u>

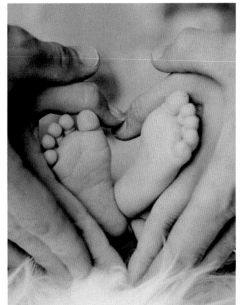

Family

HAPPINESS

To bring about change, you must not be
afraid to take the first step.
We will fail when we fail to try."
— Rosa Parks

WEALTH

"All our dreams can come true, if we have the courage to pursue them."
— <u>Walt Disney</u>

CAREER

Business

Goals

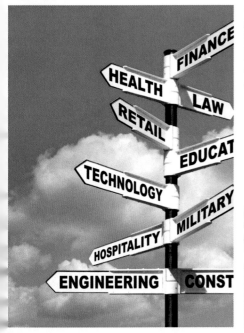

"Don't sit down and wait for the opportunities to come. Get up and make them."
— Madam C.J. Walker

TRAVEL

Champions keep playing until they get it right."
— Billie Jean King

Believe in Yourself

"I am lucky that whatever fear I have inside me, my desire to win is always stronger."
— Serena Williams

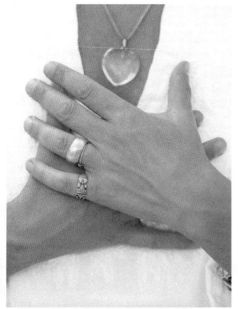

Proud
of ME

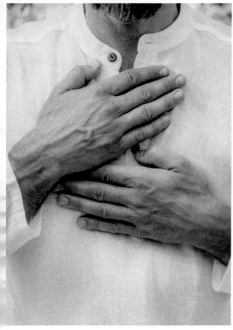

BE YOU
DO YOU
FOR YOU

"You are never too old to set another goal or to dream a new dream."
— C.S. Lewis

It is during our darkest moments that we must focus to see the light."
— Aristotle

Invest in your health!

Healthy life

GOOD
♥
HEALTH

Debt
Management
Plan

Believe you can and you're halfway there."
— Theodore Roosevelt

DO IT

F⊙CUS

We can do it!

DO
DO

Focus on your priorities!

"Life shrinks or expands in proportion
to one's courage."
— Anaïs Nin

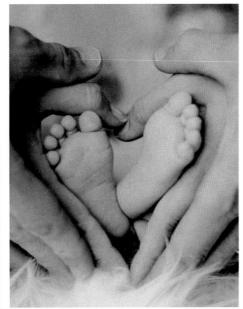

FITNESS

HEALTHY

BODY

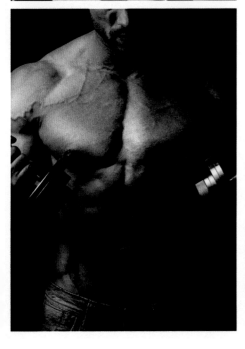

Try to be a rainbow in someone's cloud."

— Maya Angelou

If you don't like the road you're walking, start paving another one."
— Dolly Parton

Today, I will.

Setting
GOALS

CONNECT
PRESENT

"Real change, enduring change, happens one step at a time."
— Ruth Bader Ginsburg

All dreams are within reach. All you have to do is keep moving towards them."
— <u>Viola Davis</u>

It is never too late to be what you
might have been."
— George Eliot

THE FUTURE IS EXCITING..

Give light and people will find the
way."
— Ella Baker

"It always seems impossible until it's done."
— Nelson Mandela

DON'T

QUITE

TRUST

THE PROCES

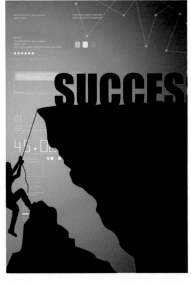

SUCCES

DON'T GIVE UP!

DECISION

Don't count the days, make the days count."

— <u>Muhammad Ali</u>

Marriage

If you risk nothing, then you risk everything."
— Geena Davis

MY DREAM HOUSE

Thank you

Congratulations on taking a powerful step toward creating the life of your dreams! May your vision board book serve as a canvas for your greatest aspirations and a daily reminder of your limitless potential.

May each image, word, and thought lead you closer to manifesting the abundant, joyful, and fulfilling life you deserve.

Here's to dreaming big, believing in yourself, and watching your vision become reality.

Wishing you success and boundless possibilities,
Ava Bliss

Made in United States
Orlando, FL
27 December 2024

56567228R00029